WHY can't I feel the EARTH SPINNING?

& other vital questions about science

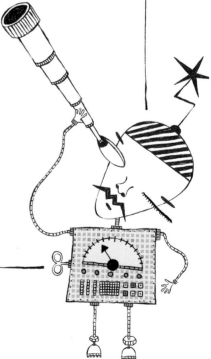

WHY can't I feel the EARTH SPINNING?

& other vital questions about science

Written by **James Doyle**

With original illustrations by **Claire Goble**

Thames & Hudson

CONTENTS

WHAT is SCIENCE?

Oh nothing much...science is everything, science is everywhere and science is everything that has ever happened in the whole history of time! Do you have a curious and inquiring mind like a scientist? Can you handle all the cool things that science can do? Are you interested in fascinating facts and mind-blowing mysteries? Well, this is the book for you. *Why can't I feel the earth spinning?* answers all the science questions you've ever asked and much, much more! From the tiniest bacteria to the biggest black holes. From the most microscopic creatures to the largest beasts that ever roamed the Earth. From the inside of your body to the furthest parts of the Universe, this book is unlike any other science book you have ever read. With that in mind, I have one last question for you. What are you waiting for?

How do we know about the Universe?

There are more than 100 billion stars in our galaxy alone. We can't land on them, or even travel to them, but we have found ways to study the Universe. In 1609, Galileo built his own telescope and used it to look at the Universe. Since then, we have discovered more than we could ever have imagined about our neighbors, the stars, moons and planets around us.

Girl looking through a large refracting telescope

How do scientists study things they can't see?

Scientists can study very small things, which are invisible to the human eye, using a microscope. A microscope lets us zoom in and see details in the things around us—small patterns on objects, tiny living things called microbes, and even the building blocks called "molecules" that make up everything. This picture of a water beetle's front foot is taken with a microscope. You can see that it is made up of tiny circles in complicated patterns and it has little hairs and circular pads that cushion its foot.

Microscopic image of a water beetle's foot

Can I become a scientist, too?

Yes, of course. Anyone who works hard and asks lots of questions has the skills to become a scientist. Many of the world's most famous scientists started out on very different paths—Stephen Hawking began by studying math but changed to physics. The astronaut Mae C. Jemison originally thought she would become a fashion designer! Anyone who questions the world can become a scientist.

Why are TREES GREEN?

Because trees REFLECT green light from the SURFACE of their leaves.

All the cells that make up a tree's leaves contain tiny little packets of **chlorophyll**. Chlorophyll helps a plant **turn light from the sun into food.** When light hits the chlorophyll in the leaves, it absorbs red and blue light and **reflects green light.** This is why trees usually look green.

In autumn, the sun is weaker and so **trees produce less food.** The green chlorophyll in the leaves starts to break down, turning the color of the leaves from green to yellow to orange and finally to brown.

The canopy of a lime tree

LOOK
at these
hard-working
leaves

What do plants eat?
Go to page 16

Trees are often known as "the **Earth's lungs.**" When animals and humans breathe in air, we absorb the oxygen and breathe out a gas called carbon dioxide, or CO_2. Trees do the opposite, they breathe in CO_2 and breathe out oxygen. **All living things need each other to survive.**

Plants combine the carbon, from the carbon dioxide they breathe in, with water from the soil and sunlight to **make sugar.** They discard the leftover oxygen into the air. This process is called **photosynthesis.**

HOW TALL IS THE TALLEST TREE?

G iant redwoods, or *sequoia sempervirens*, can easily grow to 300 feet tall. These record-breaking trees are usually found in California, in the United States of America. In 2006, a giant redwood nicknamed "Hyperion" was measured at 379.6 feet high and has been declared the world's tallest tree.

A typical redwood lives for 500 to 700 years, although some have survived for over 2,000 years!

Botanists taking a sample from a 351-foot giant redwood

CAN TREES GROW ANYWHERE?

Trees grow all over the Earth, in almost any climate. But above a certain line, or height above sea level, they stop growing.

This line is called the treeline or timberline and no trees grow above it. It is usually a point where there simply isn't enough air, heat or water to keep trees alive. From a distance the treeline looks very abrupt, as if someone has mown the top of the mountain. In reality, the line is not so abrupt. The trees get smaller and die out gradually.

Mont Sainte-Victoire, Paul Cézanne, 1902-6

HOW DO YOU KNOW HOW OLD A TREE IS?

There is a scientific method of dating a tree called dendrochronology. By counting its rings, you can calculate a tree's age exactly. Each ring marks a complete cycle of the seasons, or one year in the tree's life.

Dendrochronology is useful for studying historical changes in the environment. Trees can help us to study periods of drought or flood. The rings in trees can also tell us the amount of carbon gas in the air at a particular point in time or even when the last ice age was.

Cross-section of a 57-year-old Douglas fir tree trunk

HOW **DO** WE **KNOW** what DINOSAURS LOOKED LIKE?

Have you ever seen a LIVING DINOSAUR?

No? Nor has any other human being! Dinosaurs had been **extinct** for around **65.5 million years** before the first humans appeared on Earth. To find out about them, we are reliant on scientists who have found individual dinosaur bones set in rocks called **fossils**, and sometimes their complete skeletons. By studying dinosaur bones, scientists can work out what they looked like and how they moved all those years ago.

WHERE → do you go to meet dinosaurs?

Dinosaurs were first recognized as a group of **ancient animals** by British scientist Richard Owen in 1842. He introduced the name *Dinosauria*, which means **"terrible lizards."** At that time, scientists had uncovered the fossils of just three types of dinosaur—*Iguanodon, Hylaeosaurus* and *Megalosaurus*. Today, more than **500 different species** have been named. And there are hundreds more groups still to be discovered!

A group of children sketch an *Iguanodon* skeleton on a visit to the Natural History Museum, London

HOW ARE DINOSAURS NAMED?

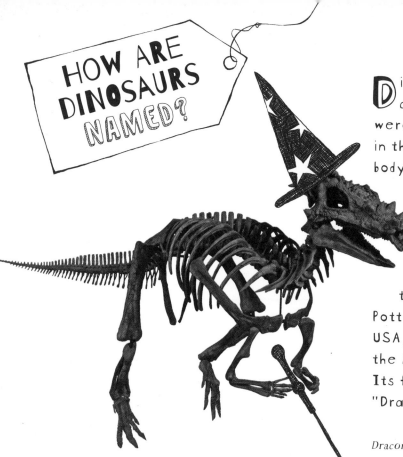

Dinosaurs are often named after the place where they were found, a person involved in the discovery, or a specific body feature. The name is usually made up of two Greek or Latin words, or a combination of both. However, the scientist who discovered *Dracorex hogwartsia* named the dinosaur after Harry Potter. It was discovered in Iowa, USA, in 2004, and is a member of the *Pachycephalosaurus* family. Its full name is grandly titled "Dragon King of Hogwarts."

Dracorex hogwartsia reconstruction

DO HOBBITS EXIST?

Yes, but not as you know them! Until 2001, scientists believed that *Homo sapiens* (that's us!) were the only human species on Earth. Our ancient cousins, the Neanderthals, died out some 30,000 years ago. However, the discovery of a skeleton just over three feet tall on the Indonesian island of Flores, from between 100,000 and 60,000 years ago, proves other human species existed before Neanderthals. The skeleton was named the "Flores Hobbit," or *Homo floresiensis*, after J.R.R. Tolkien's fictional Hobbits, who were short.

Film still of Bilbo Baggins from
The Hobbit: An Unexpected Journey, 2012

WHY ARE DINOSAURS EXTINCT?

The Cretaceous-Tertiary extinction, or K-T event, is the name given to the event that killed the dinosaurs. It happened some 65 million years ago. Scientists thought K-T might have been due to a change in temperature, which interrupted the dinosaurs' food supply. But in the 1980s scientists Luis and Walter Alvarez discovered a layer of a material called iridium in the Earth's crust. It was created at exactly the same time as the dinosaurs died. Iridium is usually found in Space, which suggests that a comet or asteroid crashed into Earth, killing the dinosaurs.

Asteroid approaching Earth, imagined illustration

What do PLANTS EAT?

Plants make some of their own food from CARBON DIOXIDE in the air.

A plant's leaves absorb carbon dioxide, or CO_2, from the air and turn it into **food** during a process called photosynthesis (see p.9). To stay healthy and strong, they also take in other **nutrients and minerals** through their **roots**.

All living things need a mineral called **nitrogen**. We absorb nitrogen through the air we breathe but plants absorb theirs from the **soil**.

POP CORN

HAVE you ever seen a plant like this?

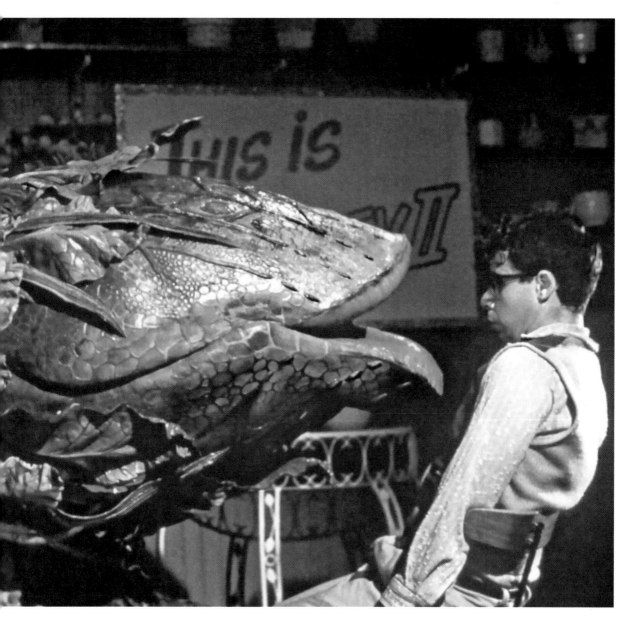

Film still from *Little Shop of Horrors*, 1986, featuring Audrey II, the man-eating plant

When plants rot and decompose, or are eaten by animals and pooed out, nothing is wasted. The useful minerals and nitrogen that a plant absorbs in its lifetime are returned to the soil, ready to be sucked up through the roots of another plant. This is the basis for what scientists call the **nitrogen cycle**.

DO PLANTS EAT ANIMALS?

Yes! There are lots of carnivorous, or meat-eating, plants such as Venus flytraps and pitcher plants. These plants grow in places that have poor soil. They get their nutrients by catching and eating insects instead of absorbing nutrients from the ground like other plants.

Finding enough food can be tricky so sometimes, instead of one species eating the other, they work together. The frog in this picture is using the pitcher plant to protect it from predators. In return, the pitcher gets to eat the frog's nutrient-rich poo. What a good deal!

A frog sitting inside the rim of a pitcher plant

WHY DO FLOWERS SMELL?

For thousands of years, humans have loved the look and smell of flowers. But it was only recently that scientists discovered what gives flowers their scent. In 1953, chemists thought that a rose's scent was made up of 20 chemicals. By 2006, it was discovered that there are closer to 400!

Not every flower smells as good as a rose. Many give off smells that you wouldn't want in a perfume. The *titan arum*, or "corpse flower," is said to smell similar to rotting flesh.

Boy with peg on his nose. Not all flowers smell good!

WHY DO BEES LOVE FLOWERS?

Bees and flowers both benefit from bee visits. The flowers use bright colors and beautiful fragrances to attract the bees.

Bees eat and collect the flower's sugary nectar and sweet-smelling, powdery pollen. While the bee feeds, pollen sticks to its body. When the bee moves to another flower for more nectar and pollen, some of the pollen from the first flower rubs off. Flowers use the pollen to create new seeds.

Pollen-covered honeybee collecting nectar

WHY do I HAVE to WASH?

Have you thought about what would happen if you NEVER WASHED again?

You would be very smelly and it could even be fatal!

Think about this: your body is covered in about six-and-a-haf square feet of skin, which contains around 2.6 million sweat glands. Your skin is also covered in thousands of tiny hairs. You **sweat constantly** from the glands all over your body. Although sweat itself has no smell, the **bacteria found on your skin** can live in your sweat and produce an **unpleasant smell.** If you don't wash, over time your skin and hair will get sticky with sweat and gunge.

Boys scrub themselves clean at camp

HOW
often do you wash?

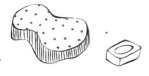

Germs live on your skin too. Normally, germs are no major threat to our health as long as they remain on the skin's surface. But if they **reach your bloodstream** it can be quite a different story. If you didn't wash in a while you would become itchy, which could send you into a **scratching frenzy**. There is serious bacteria hanging around in all that grime, such as *staphylococcus*. If that were to enter your bloodstream through the open scratches you **could die!**

Magnified eyelash mites on a human face

CAN THINGS LIVE ON MY FACE?

Disgusting, but yes! It is very likely that there are creatures living on your face at this very moment. There are two species in particular—*Demodex folliculorum* and *Demodex brevis*. These tiny creatures, or mites, love the oily and warm conditions on a face, and are related to insects and crabs.

Scientists have known that humans carry mites for a long time. *Demodex folliculorum* was spotted in human earwax in 1842. More recently, in 2014, research showed that around 14 per cent of people had face mites invisible to the human eye. Every face tested showed traces that mites had lived there at some point.

WHY DOES MY SKIN FALL OFF?

It is completely natural to shed skin. Most animals do it and snakes regularly shed old skin when a new layer of skin has developed beneath. Likewise, the human body is constantly working, building and repairing itself.

Humans shed on average about 600,000 particles of skin or skin cells every hour. That may not seem like a big deal but with a little math we can work out that a 70-year-old will have lost around 110 pounds of skin in their lifetime. To help you visualize that amount of skin—a lifetime of skin shedding would weigh as much as 150 cans of soup!

A rat snake beginning to shed its skin.

CAN FOOD CHANGE MY BODY AND SKIN?

What you eat affects your body. The vitamins and minerals in food can have a big impact. There's one food, however, that can have a deadly impact—polar bear's liver. Early Arctic explorers ate polar bear's liver without realising it was jam-packed with vitamin A. Too much vitamin A can be poisonous to humans. The explorers suffered full-body skin loss and comas, and some even died after they ate it.

Engraving of Dutch sailors on an Arctic expedition, 1596-97.

Are MAPS ALWAYS RIGHT?

No. Some maps are completely WRONG!

However, it doesn't always mean a map isn't useful just because it's inaccurate. One hugely important, but inaccurate map of the world was created using the discoveries of Greek scientist **Ptolemy** between 100 and 170 CE.

This world map combines different kinds of scientific knowledge. It used the stars to locate countries and oceans and so could be understood by people all over the world. It also **helped other mapmakers** work out the size of the Earth.

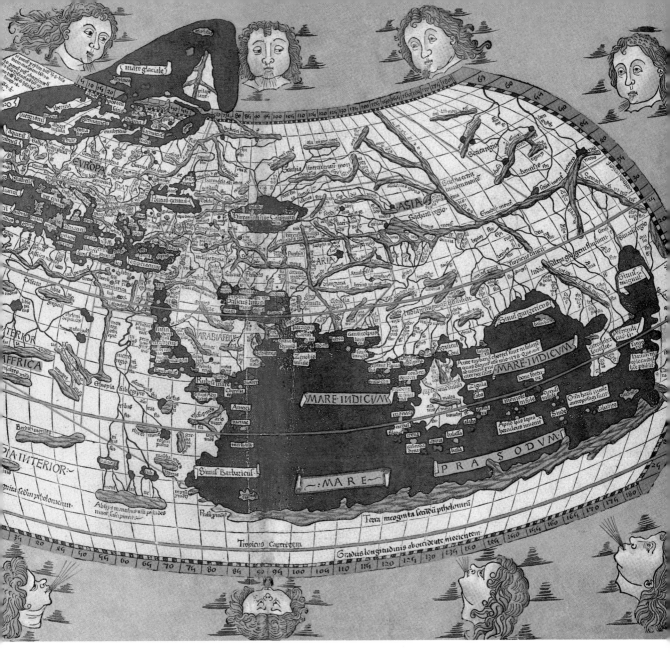

A 15th-century illustrated map based on Ptolemy's ideas

LOOK at the world map in your atlas. Does it look like this?

Ptolemy's discoveries were **lost for hundreds of years** and weren't rediscovered until **1407**. At that time, mapmakers based the size of countries on their importance and **not on their actual size**. Until Ptolemy's map of the world was rediscovered, the more important a country was, the **bigger it appeared** on the map.

CAN LIGHT GO AROUND CORNERS?

Yes, light travels in waves that can bend around corners. In fact, light always bends around corners to some extent. It can also travel in straight lines, proven by the invention of the camera obscura. This simple device was used to project images through a hole and onto a surface before film cameras were invented. At its most basic, the camera obscura is a box with a small hole in one side. Light from outside the box passes through the hole and lands on the inside wall. The result is a projection of the scene outside the box onto a screen on the inside of the box.

Copper engraving of a camera obscura. 1671

HOW DO MY EYES WORK?

Your eyes work just like a telescope. They even have a similar kind of clear lens that focuses the rays of light from objects onto the back of your eyes to create a picture.

Telescopes are better at focusing than the naked eye. They can help improve the sharpness of an image and see things a long way away. The Hubble Space Telescope is based in Space and has seen a galaxy 13.4 billion light years away!

A 17th-century engraving of an astronomer looking at the stars

WHY CAN'T I SEE MY OWN EYES?

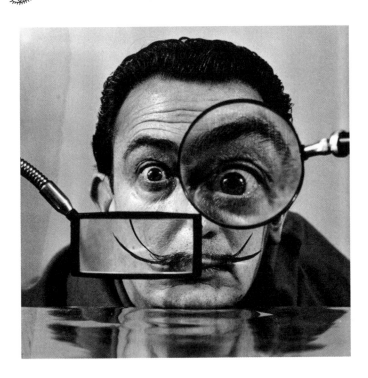

Because they are busy taking in images from the world around you. Your eyes work in a very similar way to a camera. Within the eye, the iris works like the hole in a camera, which opens and shuts when it captures a picture. The iris, which is the colored part of your eye, adjusts the amount of light entering the eye through the pupil, which is the black part. This adapts to the brightness of the place around you.

The surrealist artist Salvador Dalí, 1951

WHY does MY HAIR GROW?

Your hair and nails grow because of a PROTEIN called KERATIN.

Keratin begins life as a cell in your skin. It pushes upwards through the skin, dies and hardens. It is at this point that it turns into **hair if it is on your head, or nails if it is on your fingers or toes.**

A healthy body will produce a lot of keratin and strong, smooth nails, but an ill body will produce dry, brittle and flaky nails.

HAVE→ your nails ever been this long?

Eating meat, dairy products and pulses is great for your nails and hair. Your body breaks them down into **amino acids,** which make up different proteins including keratin. Your nails and hair grow faster and stronger when they get vitamin D from the sun. This is why they grow more in the summer than in winter.

Your hair grows about **four times as fast** as your nails at around 12 cm a year. Nails usually grow about 3 cm a year.

Shock-headed Peter, illustrated by Heinrich Hoffmann, 1847

IS MY HAIR STRONG ENOUGH TO CLIMB?

Human hair is not as strong as steel but is similar in strength to aluminium, reinforced glass fibres or Kevlar, the material that is used to make bulletproof vests.

A single strand of hair can hold 3 ½ oz. In theory, a full head of hair could support the weight of two elephants!

Rapunzel, illustrated by Margaret Evans Price, 1910

WHAT DOES MY TONGUE
SAY ABOUT ME?

Your tongue is covered in taste buds arranged in a pattern. No one else shares the same tongue print as you! Your fingers and toes have unique prints too! Fingerprints are more specific to us than DNA - the genetic material in each of our cells. The police use fingerprints to help them solve crimes.

Physicist Albert Einstein sticking out his tongue

HOW LONG ARE MY BLOOD VESSELS?

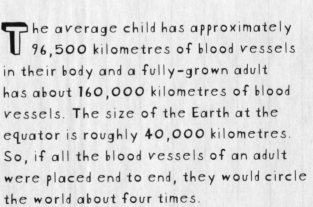

The average child has approximately 96,500 kilometres of blood vessels in their body and a fully-grown adult has about 160,000 kilometres of blood vessels. The size of the Earth at the equator is roughly 40,000 kilometres. So, if all the blood vessels of an adult were placed end to end, they would circle the world about four times.

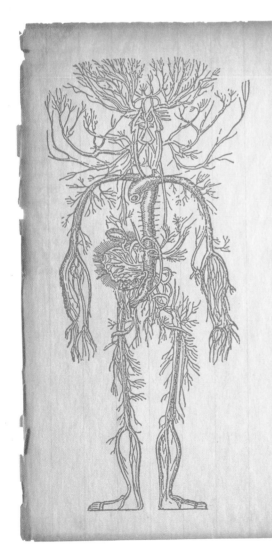

Historical illustration of the blood vessels in a human body

WHY does MEDICINE taste SO BAD?

Most of the CHEMICALS in medicine are plant-based, so are naturally BITTER to taste.

The problem lies with the taste buds on your tongue, which is covered in taste receptor cells. While there are only a few receptors for sweet flavors, nature has given us around 27 **receptors for bitterness.**

In prehistoric times, this sensitivity to bitterness stopped early humans from eating deadly plants. It was an essential **survival mechanism** that alerted the human body to dangerous toxins. Anyone who chewed these plants would naturally **spit them out** and avoid getting poisoned.

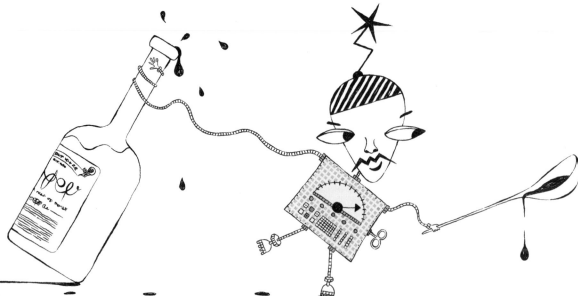

A school teacher gives her children a
spoonful of medicine, 1931

DOES

**your
medicine
taste nice?**

Children naturally **prefer** sweet
flavors. It is not until later on
in our teenage years that our
tastes change. Scientists are still
uncertain of the exact cause for
this change. One theory is that
as **the body's growth slows down,**
it needs fewer calories, and so
it stops craving sugar.

CAN PLANTS BE DEADLY?

Many plants are poisonous to humans. Even in small doses, deadly nightshade can cause horrible fevers and make you imagine things. The poison is so effective that the ancient Romans used it on poison-tipped arrows aimed at their enemies.

Monkshood, also known as wolfsbane, is also dangerous. It was used by ancient warriors to poison the water of their enemies, often resulting in death.

Deadly nightshade and monkshood, illustrated by Johnstone, 1855

HOW **DO** YOU MAKE MEDICINE?

Some medicines are discovered by accident. The scientist Sir Alexander Fleming didn't set out to make penicillin at all.

In September 1928, Fleming returned from his vacation to discover that a strange mold called *Penicillium notatum* had contaminated his petri dishes. When he examined some samples of the dangerous bacteria called *staphylococcus aureus*, he noticed that the strange mold prevented the bacteria's normal growth. He used this mold to develop the first antibiotics.

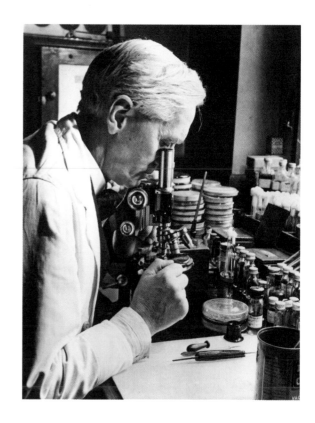

Sir Alexander Fleming in his laboratory

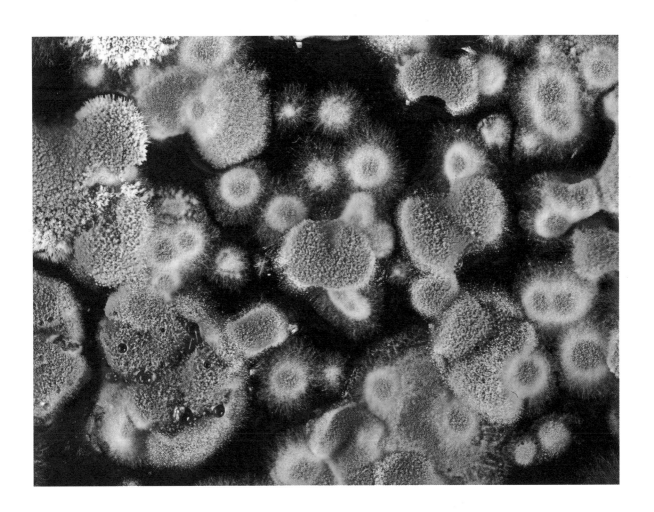

WHY CAN'T I EAT MOLD?

You can eat some molds. Have you ever tried blue Stilton cheese? The blue and gray spots are mold. It is ok to eat, but lots of other molds are extremely harmful.

In the 1840s, the Great Famine in Ireland killed around 1 million people. The culprit was *Phytophthora infestans*, or potato blight, which is a bit like a fungus. It withered leaves and rotted vegetables. Eating infected food can make people very unwell and even kill them. Many people starved because there was little else to eat.

Mold on a glass of red wine

HOW DO SURGEONS know what to TAKE OUT?

Doctors in ancient Greece used to CUT OPEN executed criminals to see how their bodies worked.

The corpses were examined by students attending the first **school of anatomy**, more than 2,300 years ago. Even before that, more than 3,500 years ago, people in ancient Egypt started making records about our bodies. **Ancient Egyptians** were the first people to identify the heart, liver, kidneys and other body parts.

By the 1100s, all students studying medicine had to learn about **human anatomy and surgery**. The students would watch a **real dead body being dissected**.

DO they look like they know what they're doing?

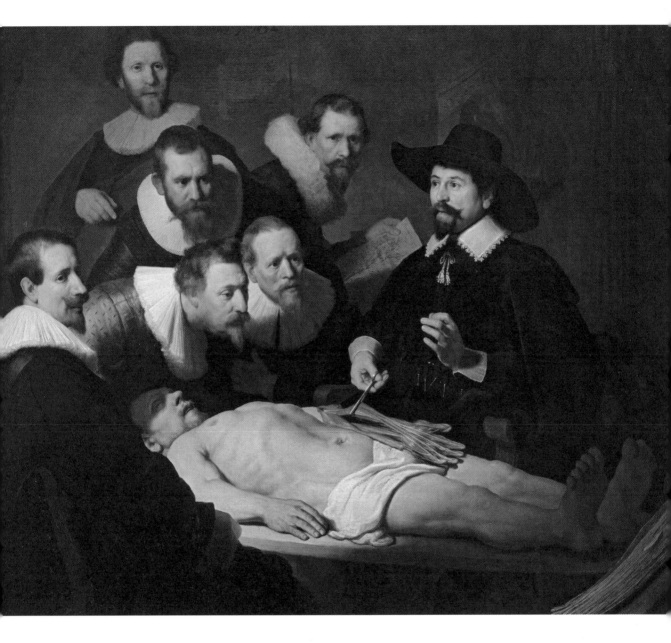

The Anatomy Lesson of Dr Nicolaes Tulp,
Rembrandt, 1632

Medical students today still practice on real bodies, but they also use plastic models. The development of super-powerful scanners, microscopes and even robot surgeons has allowed **medical advances** build on the great discoveries of the past. The combination of thousands of years of research and modern medical technology mean our surgeons **know exactly where** everything goes!

Why does medicine taste so bad?
Go to page 32

WHO DO SURGEONS PRACTICE ON?

In the 17th and 18th centuries, surgeons and students practiced on corpses, or cadavers. That is, dead bodies!

A rather nasty trade grew – BODY SNATCHING. People were paid to sneak into graveyards, dig up corpses and sell them to anatomy schools. It was big business, but highly illegal.

Film still from *The Body Snatcher*, 1945

CAN SCIENTISTS BE ARTISTS TOO?

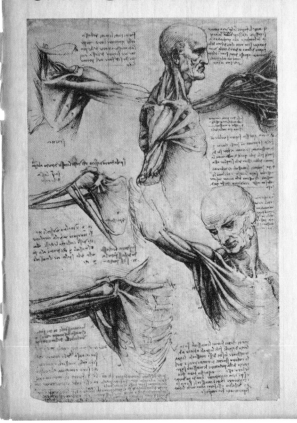

Yes they can. Leonardo da Vinci is the "father" of modern medical illustrations as well as being one of the most famous painters ever. His best-known artworks include the *Mona Lisa* and *The Last Supper*. Da Vinci studied everything from art and music through to engineering, science and math. His anatomical drawings helped greatly advance the medical knowledge of his time. They were used by students who were studying anatomy and medicine.

The muscles of the shoulder,
Leonardo da Vinci. c. 1510–11.

HOW DO WE KNOW WHAT WE LOOK LIKE INSIDE?

For thousands of years, people have studied the human body to find out how our insides work and to discover what it looks like in there.

As far back as the 1800s, copies of male and female human bodies called "medical dummies" were created. Since that time, advances in what we know about the body have been helped by the invention of X-rays, scanners and 3D imaging.

Medical dummies with removable covers, 1601–1700

WHY is BREAD full of BUBBLES?

Because of YEAST and a process called "fermentation."

Yeast feeds on sugar. As it gobbles up the sugars that are present in flour, it "ferments" and **breaks down the sugars** into carbon dioxide gas, alcohol, flavor and energy. **Carbon dioxide** creates bubbles that cause the bread to rise. **Alcohol** is also important in the process. When alcohol is at room temperature, it is a liquid. But when it heats up, such as when bread is baked at high temperatures in the oven, alcohol begins to evaporate into gas. The gas created by the **evaporating alcohol** also helps the bread to rise.

BREAD

A busy French bakery with food on display, dough being kneaded and new loaves being baked, 1875

CAN you imagine the smell of fresh bread in this room?

Gluten also has a role to play. It gives the dough its strength and elasticity. Gluten is what helps the bread dough to **hold on to the gases** produced during fermentation. The elastic quality of gluten allows the bread to **keep its shape as it rises**. Without gluten the gas bubbles in the dough would be lost and the bread would be flat and dense.

41

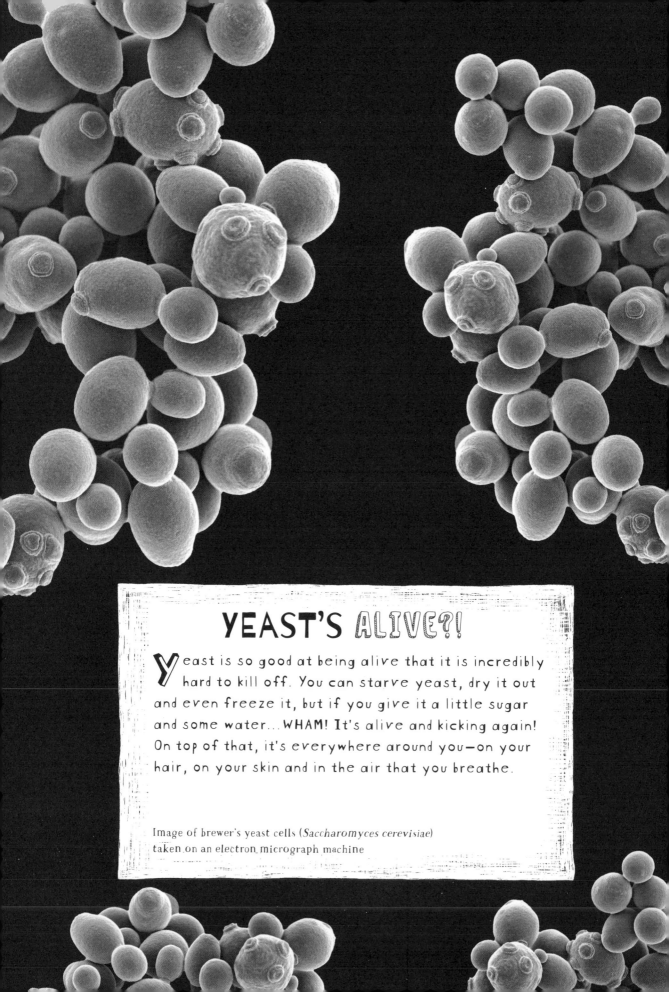

YEAST'S ALIVE?!

Yeast is so good at being alive that it is incredibly hard to kill off. You can starve yeast, dry it out and even freeze it, but if you give it a little sugar and some water...WHAM! It's alive and kicking again! On top of that, it's everywhere around you—on your hair, on your skin and in the air that you breathe.

Image of brewer's yeast cells (*Saccharomyces cerevisiae*) taken on an electron micrograph machine

WHO INVENTED BREAD?

Up until ancient Egyptian times, bread was eaten in an "unleavened" state. This means that it was a flat bread like the naan or pitta breads we eat today. Then around **4,000** years ago the Egyptians discovered a type of yeast that they called "barn." When the yeast was added to bread dough they noticed it made the bread rise. The ancient Egyptians didn't fully understand how the yeast worked. They thought that a magical power was at work.

Ancient Egyptian tomb model showing servants grinding corn and baking bread

WHO FOUND OUT ABOUT YEAST?

Bacteria exists in most food and drink and isn't harmful to us as long as it is in small quantities. But bacteria grows quickly and can spoil food and drink in a matter of days.

In 1857, the French scientist Louis Pasteur discovered that heating wine to a temperature of 55 degrees Celsius killed the bacteria that usually made it turn sour. His process, which was later named "pasteurization," worked on other food and drinks too. Now we can drink milk, beer and fruit juice weeks after it is made.

Louis Pasteur by Albert Gustaf Aristides Edelfelt. 1885

WHY do STARS TWINKLE?

Stars appear to twinkle because we see them through THICK LAYERS of moving air in the Earth's atmosphere. Stars are so far away from us that they appear as tiny dots in the sky. When the light from stars reaches our atmosphere it is bent, or **refracted**, lots of times and in different directions. This **refraction** makes it look like the star is moving a little bit, or **winking** at us. Our eyes and brain interpret this as the star twinkling. The scientific name for this is **stellar scintillation**.

CAN you count all the stars in this picture?

Hubble Space Telescope photo of
the star-forming region LH 95 in
the Magellanic cloud galaxy

Stars viewed from **outer space** do not
twinkle because there is no atmosphere
in outer space to bend the light.

This photo was taken by the **Hubble
Space Telescope**. Usually, only the
biggest, brightest and bluest stars are
visible. But many **newly formed stars**
can also be seen in this picture. They are
dimmer and more yellow than the others.
We can also see the blue shimmer of
hydrogen gas heated by the young stars.

How was
Earth made?
Go to page 48

IS THAT A HORSE IN THE SKY?

Stars cluster together in groups called constellations. People have often tried to make sense of the shapes constellations make. Since the 14th century, maps have been made of the patterns they form in the night sky. In total, 88 constellations have been identified. Many are named after characters from Greek mythology. Can you see the winged horse Pegasus on this star chart?

Star chart showing solar orbits, phases of the Moon and constellations visible from Earth, 1670

The Moon is the brightest object in our night sky and the closest thing to Earth.

The Moon's orbit around Earth varies. At its nearest point the Moon comes as close as 225,122 miles. This position is called the perigee. The farthest away it gets is called the apogee. Here, the Moon is 252,088 miles from Earth. On average, the distance between Earth and the Moon is about 238,855 miles.

The Baron travels to the Moon in the German story
The Wonderful Adventures of Baron Munchausen

HOW CLOSE IS THE MOON?

So far, no proof has been found of past or present life on Mars. However, a lot of evidence is now building up to suggest that there was once water on the surface of Mars. Water is one of the ingredients that life needs to survive. So it might mean that microscopic life once inhabited the "Red Planet." In August 2012, NASA launched *Curiosity Rover*, which is a bit like a remote-controlled car, to drive around and find out if life ever existed on the planet. It is still there, looking!

Curiosity Rover selfie on Mars

IS THERE LIFE ON MARS?

How was THE EARTH made?

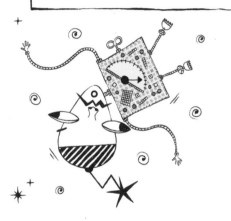

WHICH countries can you see?

Scientists believe that PLANET EARTH was made in a very hot explosion called the "BIG BANG."

This was about 13,600 million years ago. At the time, the Universe was concentrated into a **single tiny point**, which began to get bigger quickly in the hot explosion. After the Big Bang, the Universe started to **expand outwards**, with objects colliding repeatedly. These objects gradually got bigger, building up the planets in the Solar System, including Earth. The Universe is **still expanding today**, but gravity is slowing down the rate of this expansion.

A cloud-free satellite image of planet Earth

What makes thunder and lightning?
Go to page 76

Scientists have also detected a **type of radiation** called cosmic microwave background radiation or **CMBR**. This radiation is thought to be the heat that was left over from the **original Big Bang explosion**.

49

HOW IS A STAR BORN?

Stars are created out of huge cold clouds of gas and dust, known as "nebulas." The most famous of these is the Orion nebula, which is just about visible from Earth with the naked eye. These clouds, or nebulas, start to shrink under the weight of their own gravity. As the cloud gets smaller, it breaks into clumps. Each clump eventually becomes hotter and more squashed. When the temperature reaches 18 million degrees Farenheit, the clump becomes a new star.

The birthplace of stars known as the Orion nebula

WHICH STAR IS CLOSEST?

The Sun is the closest star to Earth at approximately 93 million miles away. Despite being so far away the Sun heats up Earth and supports all living things on our planet. Our next closest star neighbor is *Alpha Centauri*, which is actually three stars held together by gravity. *Alpha Centauri A and B* are two bright, close stars with a distant, dim companion named *Proxima Centauri*.

The Milky Way, the galaxy that contains our Solar System, over Yosemite Park, USA

WILL THE SUN SHINE FOREVER?

In general, stars can't shine forever. Their lifespan depends on how big they are. Our Sun is a medium-weight star so in theory, after billions of years it will turn into what is called a white dwarf star with a faint white light. Luckily, this won't happen for another 5 billion years! Bigger stars, called heavy-weight stars, have a different life cycle. They eventually blow apart in a huge explosion called a supernova and the part left behind becomes either another star or a black hole.

The Sower, Vincent van Gogh, 1888

51

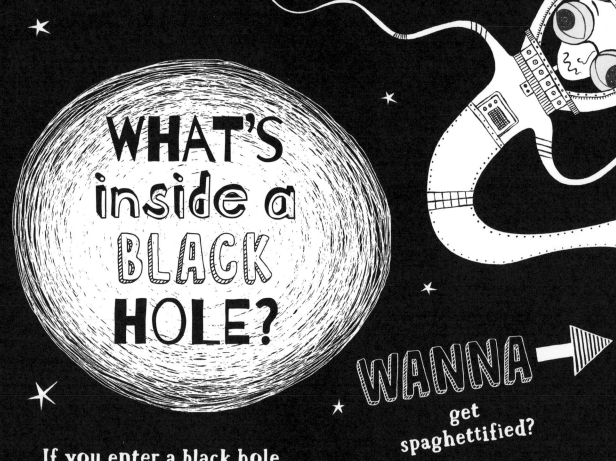

WHAT'S inside a BLACK HOLE?

WANNA → get spaghettified?

If you enter a black hole, it will be a ONE-WAY TRIP!

When a massive star burns all its fuel, it **collapses under its own weight.** If it is big enough, as it implodes, or falls in on itself, it **creates a black hole.** Around one in every thousand stars in the galaxy is **massive enough** to make a black hole.

A swirling black hole's gravity bends and warps the rays of light around it, creating a **black hole shadow.** The shadow **looks about five times bigger** than the black hole really is. You can't see the black hole itself, only its shadow, surrounded by a bright ring.

Scientists aren't sure what would happen if you actually fell into a black hole. One theory is that you would be **"spaghettified,"** that is, stretched like spaghetti and completely ripped apart.

Artist's impression of a supermassive black hole

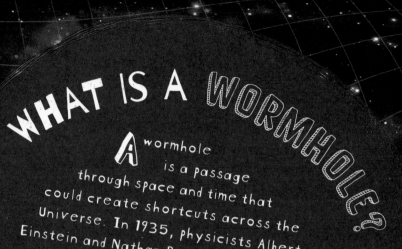

WHAT IS A WORMHOLE?

A wormhole is a passage through space and time that could create shortcuts across the Universe. In 1935, physicists Albert Einstein and Nathan Rosen suggested that wormholes might exist between points in space and time. Wormholes could be very useful for long-distance Space travel! But so far, none have been found.

Wormhole. illustrated by Mark Garlick

CAN ANYONE HEAR ME SCREAM IN SPACE?

qqqqqhhhhhhrrrrrrrrrrr ! !

In Space, no one can hear you scream, no matter how loud your voice is. This is because there is no air in Space. A space without air is called a vacuum. Sound waves cannot travel through a vacuum, so your screams cannot move from you to anyone else's ears.

This effect occurs in outer space, which begins at about 60 miles above the Earth. This is the point at which the shell of air, or atmosphere, around our planet disappears.

The Scream, Edvard Munch, c. 1893

WHAT IS THE UNIVERSE MADE OF?

Everything we can see, smell or touch, including planets and stars, is made of matter. Some matter is made up of tiny particles called atoms. It's atoms that make the Earth and the Sun pull towards one another under the effect of gravity. But only about 15 per cent of matter is made up of atoms. Scientists think that everything else is made of "dark matter." No one knows what dark matter is, because they've never seen it! But we know it exists because of the effects it has on other matter.

The Large Hadron Collider, a powerful particle accelerator

WHY DO SIRENS SOUND weird when they GO PAST?

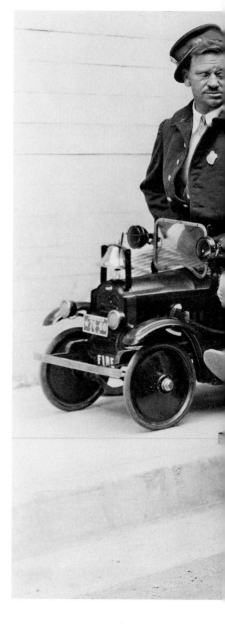

It's not just SIRENS that sound strange, it's any PASSING SOUND.

Sound travels in waves that travel away from their source. **High-pitched** sounds travel in waves that vibrate up and down quickly. **Low-pitched** sounds travel in waves that vibrate more slowly.

When the **source of a sound moves**, like when a fire engine drives towards you, the sound waves reach you faster, so the siren sounds **higher in pitch.**

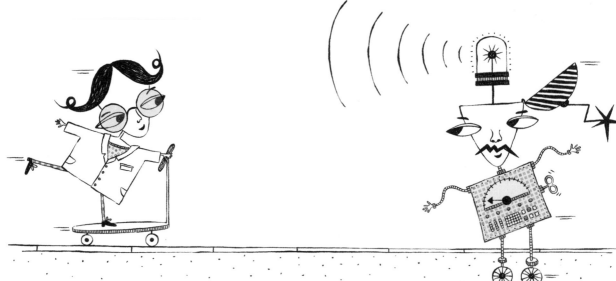

Vintage model fire engines, 1910

LISTEN
to a fire engine's siren next time it whizzes by

When the fire engine travels away from you, the sound waves take longer to reach your ear and the siren sounds **lower in pitch.**

The sound of the siren doesn't actually change—it just **appears to change**. This effect is known as the "**Doppler effect**," named after the Austrian physicist Christian Doppler, who figured this puzzle out.

It's possible to tell if a car is speeding by pointing a radar gun at it. A police officer stands at the side of the road and aims a radar gun at an approaching car. The gun sends out a burst of radio waves. The radio waves bounce off the car and back towards the radar gun at a different frequency. The radio waves will speed up in proportion to how fast the car is travelling. The faster the speed, the faster the radio wave, and the larger the speeding fine!

Renault car, c. 1900

WHAT DO SOUND WAVES LOOK LIKE?

Sound travels in waves. The problem is that these waves are invisible to the human eye. Well, they were, until the German physicist August Toepler invented a photography technique called Schlieren Flow Visualization. When a sound wave travels through the air, it changes the density, or thickness, of the air around it. Changes in air density cause light to bend—and light is something we can see. Using a combination of magnifying mirrors and a strong light, Toepler was able to capture the effect of sound waves on camera. His technique can be used to see other invisible things such as the rising heat from a candle...

A photograph of sound waves, Bell Laboratories, 1950

WHAT IS A SONIC BOOM?

A sonic boom is a loud sound, similar to an explosion. It happens when airplanes fly at the speed of sound or faster. This means that the plane is actually flying faster than the sound waves it is making. All the waves bunch up behind the plane in an extremely small space. When the "bunched up" waves reach the ground, they are heard all at once as an unmistakable boom. They also cause vibrations on the ground. This is why supersonic airplanes - airplanes faster than the speed of sound - are not allowed to fly over areas where people live.

F/A-18E Super Hornet breaks the sound barrier

How do AIRPLANES STAY UP?

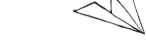

Most planes are made of METAL and are as BIG as several houses.

So how do they stay in the air? It's all to do with **lift, weight, thrust and drag.**

Lift pushes the airplane upwards. The **wings of a plane are shaped** to make air move faster over the top of the wing, and slower underneath. When air speeds up, the pressure is lowered. This means there is more pressure underneath the wings than above them, which **lifts the wing up** into the air.

HOW
is this
possible?!

Weight pulls the airplane back towards Earth. Planes are built so that their weight is spread evenly from front to back. This keeps the plane **equally balanced.**

Sometimes a plane engine uses a propeller or a jet engine to **thrust** the plane forwards. This ensures that air keeps passing over the wings, creating more lift. Finally, **drag slows the plane**. A plane flies when all four of these **forces work together.**

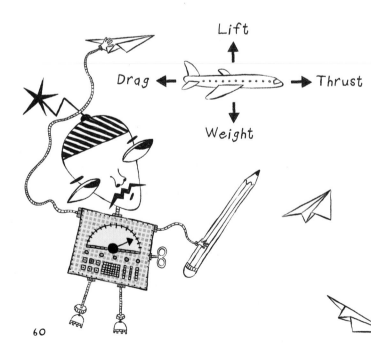

Lift
Drag ← → Thrust
Weight

An airplane flying above a British camp in the Arctic, illustrated by Leslie Carr, 1928

Cars can fly, but not very well. *Chitty Chitty Bang Bang* made flying in a car look easy, but really there is enormous difficulty in combining car design with airplane design. Their mechanical features are very different. One needs to be light and stay in the air, the other needs to be safe and stay on the ground. So yes, we can make a flying car, but it won't be a very good plane, and it won't be a very good car.

Film still from *Chitty Chitty Bang Bang*, 1968

CAN CARS FLY?

HOW DO OBJECTS MOVE?

Isaac Newton came up with three "laws of motion" that help to explain the science behind moving objects:

1. If an object, like a ball, is not already moving, it can't start moving by itself. If an object is moving, it can't stop or change direction unless something pushes it.

2. Objects will move further and faster when they are pushed harder.

3. Finally, when an object is pushed in one direction, there will always be a resistance of the same size in the opposite direction.

A red ant pushing a boulder uphill

WHY DO WE SAY "MAD AS A HATTER"?

There is a very old illness called "mad-hatter" disease. The name came from the outbreak of mercury poisonings that drove mad the specialists in the hat industry. These specialists were called "hatters." Mercury was used to treat the felt and fur used on the hats. When mental illness was recognized to be linked to their trade, the phrase "mad as a hatter" was born. It is thought that Isaac Newton was driven mad in later life by mercury poisoning from his chemical experiments.

Alice in Wonderland's Mad Hatter, illustrated by John Tenniel, 1889

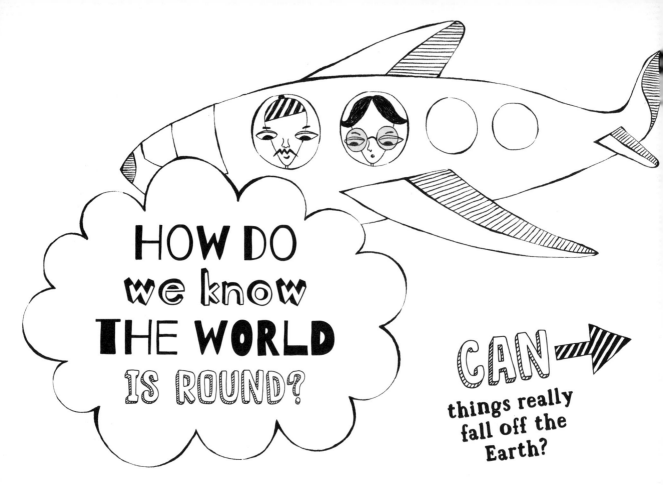

HOW DO we know THE WORLD IS ROUND?

CAN things really fall off the Earth?

In ANCIENT TIMES, people believed the Earth was FLAT. They thought that the only thing above the Earth was the sky.

In the 6th century BCE, the Greek philosopher **Anaximander** came up with the idea that Earth was like a **tin can floating in a void** – a completely empty space – and that the Sun and stars circled around it. This was a **revolution** in science because the idea was one step **closer to reality** and different to what people had previously imagined about planet Earth.

If you want to **prove the Earth is round**, one of the easiest ways is to take a long-haul flight. When you are high in the air you will notice two things. Firstly, planes can travel in straight lines for many thousands of miles and **never fall off the edge** of the planet.

Secondly, if you look out the window as you fly over the ocean, you can usually **see the curve** of the Earth along the horizon.

Fantasy map of a flat Earth illustrated by Antar Dayal

DO STARS MOVE?

Stars don't move unless they are shooting stars. Star trails, which you can see in photographs, are caused by the Earth moving and not the stars. This amazing picture was taken in the Andean Mountains in South America. The image shows the position of the stars in comparison with the rotation of the Earth during a single night. They map out circular trails as we move below them.

Whirling southern star trails over the ALMA telescope, Chile

WHY CAN'T I FEEL THE EARTH SPINNING?

At the equator, the speed of the Earth's spin is 1,040 miles per hour and yet you don't feel Earth spinning! This is because you and everything else, including the oceans, mountains and continents, are spinning along with the Earth at the same constant speed.

It's similar to flying in a plane when it is moving at a constant speed. You can almost convince yourself that you're not moving. A jumbo jet flies at about 500 miles per hour, but when you're in it, it doesn't feel as though you are moving at all.

Carousel swing ride

WHY DO ASTRONAUTS FLOAT?

Astronauts float in Space because there is very little gravity there compared to the gravity on the Earth's surface. Gravity is the force that causes every object to pull every other object towards it. Some people wrongly think that there is no gravity in Space. In fact, there is just a very small amount. Gravity is what holds the Moon in orbit around Earth and causes Earth to orbit the Sun. It keeps the Sun in place in the Milky Way galaxy. And it keeps us on the Earth.

Astronaut Mark Lee jets about outside the space shuttle
Discovery, more than 120 miles above Earth

WHY is the SEA BLUE?

The sea ISN'T ALWAYS BLUE. It can be many colors and even light up.

The sea often appears to be blue because of how it **absorbs sunlight.** Red, orange and yellow bands of light are absorbed more easily by water than blue light. So when **white light** from the sun enters the ocean, it is mostly the blue that bounces off and is picked up by our eyes.

Sometimes, the ocean looks green and even red. This can be due to the **presence of algae** and plant life living in the sea. Red algae earned the Red Sea its name. The sea might appear gray if it is **under a cloudy sky**. It can look brown when the water contains a lot of silt or sand, for example after the water has been **stirred up by a storm**.

Bioluminescence from glowing plankton,
Vaadhoo island, Raa Atoll, Maldives

Strangest of all is when the **sea lights up.** This rare event was first described by sailors. They wrote about "sailing upon a field of snow" in absolute darkness with not so much as the light of the Moon. This light was probably produced by **huge colonies of glowing bacteria** in the water. The effect is called **bioluminescence.**

HAVE
you ever
seen the
sea glow?

69

WHAT LIVES AT THE BOTTOM OF THE SEA?

It is pitch black and freezing cold at the bottom of the sea because the Sun's rays can't travel that far through the water. Despite this, creatures still inhabit these dark depths. Species such as the giant squid, the angler fish and the squidworm have adapted to thrive in these conditions. The squidworm has ten tentacle-like "arms" on its head, which are each longer than its whole body. It uses these to collect particles of food that drift down from the ocean above. At this depth, animals have to deal with crushing pressure and freezing temperatures. Many have a type of anti-freeze in their bodies to stop them from freezing to death.

A squidworm swimming at a depth of 9,180 feet in the Celebes Sea

CAN YOU LIVE IN A SUBMARINE?

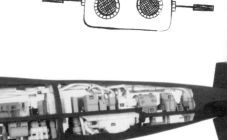

You can live in a submarine for quite a long time. Many of the world's navies can stay underwater in submarines for around three months at a time. Air for breathing is not a problem because the sailors recycle the air they breathe and make their own fresh oxygen. The limit to how long people can stay underwater is determined by how long the food and supplies can last.

Cross-section model of a military submarine

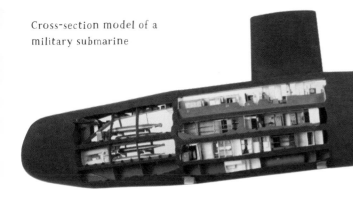

HOW DO YOU GET TO THE BOTTOM OF THE SEA?

Without a vessel like a submarine, it is impossible for a human to get to the bottom of a deep sea. The pressure of the water on top of us would crush us. However, we can go pretty deep with the right equipment. Long before spacesuits were invented, we had diving suits. The first known diving helmet was invented by the astronomer Edmond Halley in the late 17th century. It was basically a large metal helmet that was supplied with air through a tube to allow the diver to breathe.

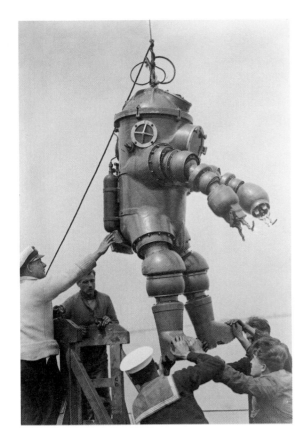

A diving suit undergoes deep-sea tests, 1933

WHERE do MOUNTAINS COME FROM?

Mountains are made by POWERFUL MOVEMENTS of the Earth's surface.

There are four types of mountain, which are formed in different ways. The most common are **fold mountains**. These are created when two enormous **tectonic plates** in the Earth's crust crash into one another, causing the edges of the plates to crumple and fold, pushing the land upwards. Some of the highest peaks, including the Himalayas, were formed in this way.

Volcanic eruptions can also produce mountains. Repeated eruptions along fault lines, or areas where the Earth's tectonic plates meet, can cause **molten rock and ash** to spew out from inside the Earth. The molten rock builds up and hardens over time to form mountains.

HAVE you ever seen a volcano erupt?

Dome mountains are the third type. These form when molten rock below the Earth's crust increases in pressure, and pushes the surface upwards. This makes rounded-shaped mountains.

Finally, mountains can be made when two plates push together. Instead of folding, they crack, and a huge chunk of rock is pushed up to create what is known as a **block mountain**.

The Klosters Mountains, Ernst Ludwig Kirchner, c. 1923

How was the Earth made? Go to page 48

Mauna Kea is a volcanic island in the Pacific Ocean. It belongs to the chain of islands that make up Hawaii. Mauna Kea is 13,795 feet tall. This makes it much lower than Mount Everest, which at 29,028 feet is generally thought to be the tallest mountain on Earth.

But there's a catch! These measurements are taken from the sea level to the top of the mountain. This puts Mauna Kea at a big disadvantage, since most of it is under water. If the height of Mauna Kea was measured from its base on the ocean floor, it would be more than 32,808 feet tall—which would make it the world's tallest mountain!

Ships off the Kohala coast, with snow-capped Mauna Kea in view, illustrated c. 1830

WHICH IS THE WORLD'S TALLEST MOUNTAIN?

WILL THERE BE NEW MOUNTAINS?

Yes, and the newest is being built right now! The Hawaiian archipelago, or island chain, lies in the middle of the Pacific Ocean. One hundred and thirty-two mountainous islands, reefs and islets rise above the surface of the water. Little Lō'ihi rises around **10,000** feet above the ocean floor but is still some **3,084** feet short of breaking through the ocean's surface. It is expected that in tens of thousands of years this little lump of lava may finally show its face.

Hot lava flowing into the Pacific Ocean

DO MOUNTAINS GET TALLER?

Clear evidence has been found to show that some mountains used to be at, or even below, sea level. Rock samples from mountain ranges such as the Himalayas and the Andes have been found to contain sea shells dating back **18,000** years. Scientists believe that the world's highest mountain, Everest, is still growing. Currently measured at **29,028** feet, it is possible that Everest's future climbers will have a longer trek to the top than those who reached its summit in the past.

Edmund Hillary's Mount Everest expedition, 1953

What makes THUNDER and LIGHTNING?

Lightning is an ELECTRIC CURRENT created inside a thundercloud.

Thunderclouds form when warm, moist air meets colder air. The **warm air rises**, forming huge clouds. Tiny ice crystals inside the clouds crash into each other and all these tiny collisions generate **static electricity**. After a while, the whole cloud fills up with electricity. Lightning flashes are a thundercloud's way of **releasing electricity**.

HAVE you seen forked lightning?

Film Still from *King Kong*, 1933

The rumble or **cracking sound of thunder** is caused by the extreme heat and movement of air along the path of the lightning flash. When lightning strikes it makes a **hole in the air** called a "channel." After the lightning is gone, the **hole collapses**. The sound you hear when the hole collapses is the thunder. Thunderstorms are very common on Earth. It is estimated that a lightning bolt strikes somewhere on the Earth's surface approximately **100 times every second**

Is "the cloud" a real cloud?

Go to page 84

IS LIGHTNING ALWAYS MADE IN A STORM?

Lightning mostly happens inside a thunderstorm, but sometimes volcanic eruptions can create lightning, too.

Electricity is made when rock fragments, ash and ice particles crash into each other above the volcano. Static electric charges are produced in the cloud of ash, just as ice particles do in normal storm clouds.

Lightning forming around an erupting volcano

HOW HOT IS LIGHTNING?

The average temperature of a lightning bolt is extraordinarily hot. It heats the surrounding air to around 49,890°F. That is around five times hotter than the temperature on the surface of the Sun, which is estimated to be 9,941°F. Even more impressive is the fact that a single bolt of lightning can be as narrow as the width of an average mobile phone, at a tiny 2 in across.

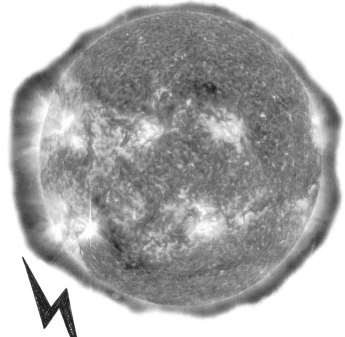

Our star, the Sun

DOES LIGHTNING EVER STRIKE TWICE?

There is a very old saying that lightning never strikes in the same place twice. But this is a complete myth.

Many places or things are struck by lightning regularly. This is especially true for tall objects, which are more likely to attract lightning because they are closer to the clouds, where the electricity is generated. For example, the Empire State Building in the United States of America is estimated to be hit nearly 25 times a year!

Lightning strikes the Empire State Building. 9 July 1957

COULD I LIVE ON MARS?

NASA wants to send ASTRONAUTS to the "RED PLANET" by 2030.

However, Mars is an extremely difficult environment for human life. It is incredibly cold and has intense radiation, which damages human's bodies.

A private company called SpaceX aims to get people there **even sooner**—by 2024.

Getting there is one thing, but **living on Mars** is another.

↑

LOOK

at your bedroom on the Red Planet!

An artist's impression of homes made in caves on Mars

Billions of years ago Mars was surrounded by an atmosphere of air and water like planet Earth. Now, the atmosphere is unbreathable for humans and is mostly made from dangerous carbon dioxide. On the positive side, Mars is covered in a concrete-like material called regolith that could be used to **make buildings**. There are also cave systems that could be converted into **underground homes** to protect people from the radiation. Founder of SpaceX, Elon Musk, aims to build a **colony** on Mars that could be home to **1 million humans**.

Why do stars twinkle? Go to page 44

VACATION IN SPACE?

It looks like summer vacations in Space might soon be a reality. People are developing spaceships that could take us to the Moon. But we're not there quite yet. Firstly, Space travel is extremely expensive. Just to launch a shuttle into Space takes **44,000** gallons of fuel. That's enough to fill up **42,000** cars. In 2001, the first Space tourist paid a whopping £15 million to spend a week in Space. Secondly, Space travel is dangerous. It requires a huge amount of speed, heat and fuel to launch through and re-enter Earth's atmosphere. But at least we don't have to worry about aliens... probably.

Extraterrestrial alien with two astronauts.
illustrated by Anton Brzezinski

HOW FAST IS A ROCKET?

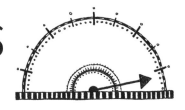

Any rocket can achieve a very high speed if it accelerates, or gathers speed, for a long time. An ordinary rocket has a hard time doing this because a huge amount of fuel is needed to journey into Space. The weight of the fuel can also make the rocket too heavy to lift off.

The minimum speed for a Space-going rocket is 27,350 mph. The further from the Earth the rocket wants to travel, the faster it needs to go. If a rocket wants to get to the Moon, it needs to travel at 41,350 mph.

A toy rocket

IS THERE REALLY A MAN ON THE MOON?

No, but sometimes the Moon looks like it has a face. The Moon was hit by a powerful asteroid billions of years ago. The impacts of the asteroid triggered volcanic eruptions on the Moon's surface. Hot lava spewed out and flooded the lunar landscape. When it cooled, it created dark patches on the Moon called "lunar maria" or "lunar seas." During a full Moon, these patches look like a grinning human face, commonly known as the "Man in the Moon."

Film still from *A trip to the Moon*, Georges Méliès, 1902

IS "THE CLOUD" a REAL cloud?

No. "THE CLOUD" describes how INFORMATION can be reached from the INTERNET.

Information no longer needs to be stored in books or on computers in the same room we are in, it can be kept on **remote servers** anywhere in the world. Cloud computing has brought about an enormous change in how we **get, save and swap information**.

Exactly "where" everything is kept can be difficult for us to understand. So the name "the cloud" makes it easier to imagine where the information is—**it is stored** up there somewhere in a fluffy "cloud" that the internet represents.

Most
of us use
"cloud" computing every
day and don't even realize it.
When you sit at a computer or use
a smartphone and type a question into
a **search engine** like Google, your device is
doing very little. **It is just a messenger**. The words
you type are rapidly fired over the internet to one of
Google's hundreds of thousands of clustered PCs, which dig
out your results and send them quickly back to you. When you do
a Google search, the real work in finding your answers might be
done by a **remote computer** sitting in California or Tokyo.

A cumulus cloud in the sky

DO

**you keep
anything in
"the cloud"?**

CAN I PLAY SOCCER WITH A ROBOT?

ASIMO is the world's most advanced humanoid robot. ASIMO stands for "Advanced Step in Innovative Mobility." It has the balance and agility to kick a football, and can run at 6 kmph. ASIMO takes part in an annual international robotics competition called RoboCup. The idea is that by 2050, a team of robotic soccer players will win a soccer game against the human winners of the most recent World Cup.

Robots compete in the RoboCup championship in Nagoya, Japan, 2017

WHY IS A "MOUSE" CALLED A MOUSE?

Douglas Engelbart invented the computer "mouse" in 1968. But to start with he called it the "X-Y position indicator for a display system," which is less catchy. When asked how his now-famous invention got the cuter name of the "mouse," Engelbart says, "No one can remember. It just looked like a mouse with a tail, and we all called it that." The wire "tail" originally came out under the user's wrist.

A wood mouse

HOW BIG IS THE BIGGEST COMPUTER EVER?

The earliest computers were hulking great machines and SAGE was by far the largest. SAGE stands for "Semi-Automatic Ground Environment." It was built in 1957, and was so big that it had to be spread across more than 20 different locations. Each part of SAGE was about the size of a football field. Despite its enormous size, SAGE had less processing power than a mobile phone. Today, computers can be smaller than a full stop on a page, and are getting ever smaller.

Early computer, 1950

WHY do I DREAM?

Dreams can be EXCITING, scary, happy, sad or just weird.

They combine images, ideas, moods and feelings. The reason we have dreams, and their purpose, is **not fully understood**. But the study of dreams does have a name. It is called "**oneirology.**"

Dreams mainly take place in the **REM**, or **rapid-eye movement**, phase of sleep. This is when brain activity is high. Our brain is almost as alert as when we are awake. During REM, our eyes move constantly even though we're asleep.

Film still of Alice and the White Rabbit in
Alice's Adventures in Wonderland, 1972

At times, dreams may happen during other stages of sleep. However, these dreams tend to be much **less memorable** or clear. People are more likely to **remember the dream** if they are woken up during the REM phase. The **average person** has between three and five dreams per night. Dreams also tend to last longer as the night progresses.

WHAT is the strangest dream you've ever had?

Sleeping Beauty, illustrated by Viktor Mihajlovic Vasnecov, 1900-26

HOW **LONG** DO WE **SLEEP** FOR?

The average human being sleeps for around eight hours each night, which is one third of a 24-hour day. In other words, we are asleep for around one third of our entire life! That means a 75-year-old has slept for approximately 25 years of their life. Not too bad—but in the original fairy tale, Sleeping Beauty is said to have slept for **100** years!

WHY DO WE SLEEPWALK?

Some people sleepwalk during deep sleep. This is much more common in children than adults and is more likely to occur if a person hasn't had enough sleep. Symptoms can range from sitting up in bed and looking around, to walking around the room or house and even going outside and driving long distances.

Doctors aren't exactly sure what causes sleepwalking but many suggest that it can be linked to the person being overly tired, being on medication or having a fever-based illness.

A man sleepwalking down a fire escape

People have often tried to work out the meaning behind dreams. Today, many scientists believe that dreams can reveal a person's hidden wishes and emotions. Other experts suggest that they are the brain's way of storing memories or problem-solving.

In ancient Greek and Roman times people believed that dreams were direct messages from the gods, messages from the dead, or that they could predict the future. In the Old Testament of the Bible, Joseph famously explains Pharaoh's dream. It predicts seven years of plenty followed by seven years of famine.

WHAT DO OUR DREAMS MEAN?

Joseph interpreting Pharaoh's dream, illustrated by Reginald Arthur, 1881–96

GLOSSARY

algae Microscopic plant life that grows in water.

altitude How high something isabove above sea level.

amino acids Chemicals used in every single cell of your body to build the proteins that you need to survive.

anatomy The study of the location of the different parts of the human body including the bones, blood vessels and organs.

antifreeze A chemical that makes it harder for water to freeze by lowering its freezing point.

antibiotics A medicine, such as penicillin, that is used to treat infections caused by bacteria.

antioxidants Vitamins and other nutrients that help to protect the cells in living things.

aperture An opening that controls how much light passes into a camera.

atmosphere The layer of gases that make up the air that surrounds the Earth or any planet.

Big Bang A theory of how the Universe began with a giant blast of matter and energy about 14 billion years ago.

bioluminescence Light given off naturally by certain kinds of insects, fish or bacteria.

chlorophyll The green substance or pigment in a plant leaf.

dark matter Invisible matter in Space that we cannot detect.

DNA Stands for deoxyribonucleic acid. DNA is the material that carries all the information about how a living thing will look and function.

electron micrograph An image similar to those created using a standard microscope but with much greatermagnification.

evolution The theory that all the kinds of living things that exist today developed from earlier types of living things.

frequency The rate at which something occursover a particular period oftime or in a given unit oftime.

gravity An invisible force discovered by Isaac Newton that makes objects falldown towards the Earth.

humanoid A robot or other artificial intelligence that has human characteristics.

islet A small island.

K-T event A large-scale mass extinction of animal and plant species that happened about 66 million years ago.

nuclear reaction A process in which two nuclei or nuclear particles collide and produce large amounts of energy.

orbit Objects in space orbit or circle around other objects. The Moon and satellites orbit the Earth, and the Earth orbits the Sun.

photosynthesis The process by which a plant turns light from the sun into food.

pigment Natural coloring in the cells of animals or plants.

pollination The transfer of pollen between flowers that fertilizes a plant and allows reproduction to happen.

predator An animal that naturally preys on other animals.

radiation Energy that moves from one place to another. Light, sound and heat are examples of radiation.

refraction The bending of light as it passes through something.

static electricity The build-up of an electrical charge on thesurface of an object.

supersonic Something that is faster than the speed of sound.

tectonic plates The Earth's crust is split into 7 parts called tectonic plates. These move around very slowly and rub against each other.

toxin A poison made by a plant or animal.

vacuum A space that contains no matter, not even air.

wavelength Light, heat and soundtravel in waves. The length between the crests of the waves , or wavelength, tells us what thelight, heat or sound will be like.

INDEX

ILLUSTRATION CREDITS

a=above, b=below

6 John R. Foster / Science Photo Library; 7(a) Igor Siwanowicz, 7(b) Will & Deni McIntyre / Getty Images; 8 Photo by Wodicka/ullstein bild via Getty Images; 10 Michael Nichols/National Geographic Creative; 11(a) The Metropolitan Musum of Art / The Walter H. and Leonore Annenberg Collection, Gift of Walter H. and Leonore Annenberg, 1994, Bequest of Walter H. Annenberg, 2002;11(b) Henri D. Grissino-Mayer, The University of Tennessee, Knoxville; 13 Harry Todd/Fox Photos/Getty Images; 14(a) Children's Museum Indianapolis;14 (b) Moviestore Collection / REX / Shutterstock; 15 Mark Garlick / Science Photo Library; 16 Photos 12 Cinema / Geffen Company / Diomedia; 18 Maximilian Weinzierl / Alamy Stock Photo; 17(a) Bettmann / Getty Images; 17(b) Adstock RF / Diomedia; 20–21 Fox Photos / Getty Images; 22 Eye of Sciene/Science Photo Library; 23(a) Heidi & Hans-Juergen Koch / Minden Pictures / Getty Images; 23(b) Photo by Chris Hellier/Corbis via Getty Images; 24–25 Wikimedia Commons; 26 akg-images; 27(a) Photo by Leemage/Corbis via Getty Images; 27(b) Photo by Willy Rizzo/ Paris Match via Getty Images; 27 Chronicle/ Alamy Stock Photo; 30 Universal Images Group / Diomedia; 31(a) Bettmann / Getty Images; 31(b) Mehau Kulyk/ Science Photo Library; 32 Photo by Fox Photos/Getty Images; 34(a) Wellcome Library, London; 34(b) Bettmann / Getty Images; 35 Shutterstock; 36 Wikicommons / Jan Arkesteijn / CC-ShareAlike; 38 Photos 12 Cinema / Photo12/ WolfTracerArchive / Diomedia; 39(a) Eric Vandeville / akg-images; 39(b) Science Museum / Science & Society Picture Library – All rights reserved; 40 Photo (C) RMN-Grand Palais (MuCEM) / Gérard Blot; 42 Steve Gschmeissner/ Science Photo Library / Getty Images; 43(a) TopFoto.co.uk / EUFD; 43(b) Heritage Image Partnership Ltd / Alamy Stock Photo; 44 Photo by Fine Art Images/ Heritage Images/Getty Images; 46(a) World History Archive / Alamy Stock Photo; 46(b) Mary Evans / Playhour; 47 NASA/JPL-Caltech/MSSS; 48 EUMETSAT / DLR; 50 NASA, ESA, M. Robberto and the Hubble Space Telescope Orion Treasury Project Team; 51(a) WIN-Initiative / Getty Images; 51(b) Fine Art Images / Diomedia; 53 NASA/JPL-Caltech; 54 Mark Garlick / Science Photo Library/Getty Images, 55(a) Universal History Archive/UIG via Getty Images; 55(b) Maximilien Brice / CERN; 56 Old Visuals / Superstock; 58(a) Buyenlarge / Getty Images 59(a) Universal Images Group / Diomedia; 59(b) Navy photo by Petty Officer 3rd Class Matthew Granito; 61 Mary Evans Picture Library; 62 Warfield/United Artists/Kobal/REX/ Shutterstock; 63(a) Antrey/Getty Images; 63(b) Heritage Images / The Print Collector/ Diomedia; 65 Antar Dayal / Getty Images; 66(a) ESO/B. Tafreshi (twanight.org); 66(b) Kristen Elsby / Getty Images; 67 Shuttle Crew STS-64, NASA; 68 Doug Perrine/Nature Picture Library/Getty Images; 70 Larry Madin / WHOI; 71(a) Dorling Kindersley / Getty Images; 71(b) TopFoto.co.uk; 72 akg-images; 74 Hawaiian Legacy Archive / Getty Images; 75(a) Don King / Getty Images; 75(b) Everett Collection Inc / Alamy Stock Photo, 76–77 Photo by Ernest Bachrach/John Kobal Foundation/Getty Images; 78 National Pictures / TopFoto; 79(a) NASA/ SDO/GSFC; 79(b) SuperStock RM/Diomedia; 80–81 ZAarchitects: Arina Agieieva, Dmitry Zhuikov; 82 Photo by Forrest J. Ackerman Collection/ CORBIS/Corbis via Getty Images; 83(a) Getty Images; 83(b) Mary Evans / Ronald Grant / Diomedia; 84 northlightimages / Getty Images; 86 Kyodo News via Getty Images; 87(a) Rudmer Zwerver / Shutterstock; 87(b) Bettmann / Getty Images; 89 Moviestore Collection/REX/ Shutterstock; 90(a) Fine Art Images / Diomedia; 90(b) Mary Evans / Classic Stock / H. Armstrong Roberts; 91 Christie's Images / Scala Archives, Florence

Text by James Doyle
Edited by Sue Grabham
Designed by Anna Perotti at By The Sky Design
Picture research by Kate Duncan

First published in 2018 in the United States of
America by Thames & Hudson Inc., 500 Fifth
Avenue, New York, New York 10110

www.thamesandhudsonusa.com

Library of Congress Control Number 2018932102

ISBN 978-0-500-65118-6

Printed and bound in China through
Asia Pacific Offset Ltd